FAMILY
Car Songbook™

RUNNING PRESS • PHILADELPHIA

Canadian representatives: General Publishing Co., Ltd.,
30 Lesmill Road, Don Mills, Ontario M3B 2T6.
International representatives: Worldwide Media Services, Inc.,
115 East Twenty-third Street, New York, NY 10010.

9 8 7 6 5 4 3 2 1
Digit on the right indicates the number of this printing.

ISBN 1–89471–996–3 (package)

Cover design by Toby Schmidt
Cover illustration by Fred Schrier
Interior illustration by Len Epstein
Spot illustration by Fred Schrier
Typography: ITC Berkeley Oldstyle by
COMMCOR Communications Corporation, Philadelphia, Pennsylvania

This book may be ordered by mail from the publisher.
Please add $2.50 for postage and handling.
But try your bookstore first!
Running Press Book Publishers
125 South Twenty-second Street
Philadelphia, Pennsylvania 19103

Contents

Over the River and through the Woods

O - ver the ri - ver and

through the woods To grand-mo-ther's house we

go. The horse knows the way to

car - ry the sleigh thru the white and drift - ed

snow - oh! O - ver the ri - ver and

through the woods Oh, how the wind doth

5

continued next page

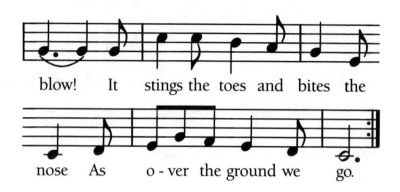

blow! It stings the toes and bites the
nose As o-ver the ground we go.

2

Over the river and through the woods
To have a real day of play.
Oh, hear the bells ring,
They ting-a-ling-ling,
Because it's Thanksgiving Da-ay.
Over the river and through the woods
Trot fast, my dappled gray.
Spring over the ground just like a hound,
For this is Thanksgiving Day.

3

Over the river and through the woods
And straight through the barnyard gate.
We seem to be go-ing ever so slow.
It's so very hard to wait!
Over the river and through the woods
Now grandmother's cap I spy.
Hurrah for fun! Are the puddings done?
Hurrah for the pumpkin pie!

America the Beautiful

Oh beau - ti - ful for spa - cious skies, For am - ber waves of grain, For pur - ple moun - tain ma - jes - ties A - bove the fruit - ed plain. A - mer - i - ca! A - mer - i - ca! God shed his grace on thee And crown thy good with bro - ther - hood

continued next page

from sea to shin - ing sea.

2

Oh beautiful for pilgrim feet
Whose stern impassion'd stress
A thoroughfare for freedom beat across
    the wilderness.
America! America! God mend thine
    every flaw,
Confirm thy soul in self-control,
Thy liberty in law.

3

Oh beautiful for heroes proved
In liberating strife,
Who more than self their country loved and
    mercy more than life.
America! America! May God thy gold refine
Till all success be nobleness
And every gain divine.

4

Oh beautiful for patriot dream
That sees beyond the years.
Thine alabaster cities gleam, undimmed by
human tears.
America! America! God shed His grace
on thee
And crown thy good with brotherhood
From sea to shining sea.

The Old Gray Mare

Oh, the old gray mare, she

Ain't what she used to be, Ain't what she

used to be, Ain't what she used to be, The

old gray mare, she Ain't what she

used to be, Ma - ny long years a - go.

Chorus: Ma - ny long years a - go,

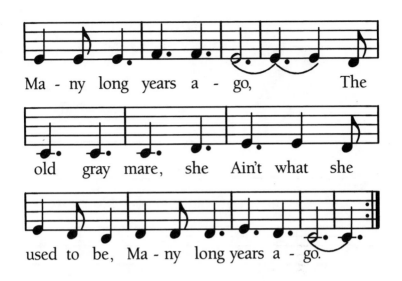

Ma - ny long years a - go, The
old gray mare, she Ain't what she
used to be, Ma - ny long years a - go.

2

Oh, the old gray mare, she
Kicked on the wiffletree,
Kicked on the wiffletree,
Kicked on the wiffletree,
The old gray mare, she
Kicked on the wiffletree
Many long years ago.

chorus

The Marines' Hymn

From the Halls of Mon - te -

zu - u - ma To the shores of Tri - po -

li, We - e fight our count - ry's

ba - at - tles In the air, on land, and

sea. First to fight for right and

free - e - dom And to keep our ho - nor

clean, We are proud to claim the ti -

i - tle Of U - ni - ted States Ma - rine.

2

Our flag's unfurled to every breeze
From dawn to setting sun.
We have fought in every clime and place
Where we could take a gun.
In the snow of far-off northern lands
And in sunny tropic scenes,
You will find us always on the job –
The United States Marines.

3

Here's health to you and to our Corps
Which we are proud to serve.
In many a strife we've fought for life
And never lost our nerve.
If the Army and the Navy
Ever look at Heaven's scenes
They will find the streets are guarded
By United States Marines.

Greensleeves

A - las, my lo - ve! You

do me wr - ong To cast me o - ff dis -

court-eous-ly. For I have l - ov - ed

you so lo - ng, De - li - ght - ing

i - n your com - pa - ny.

Green-sle-eves was all my j - o - y.

Green-sleeves w - a - s my de - light.

Green-sleeves was my heart of go - ld, Yea,

who but my la - a - dy Green-sleeves?

2

I have been ready at your hand,
To grant whatever that you might crave.
I have wagered both life and land,
Your love and good-will for to have.
If you intend thus to disdain,
It doth the more enrapture me.
And even so, I still remain
Your lover in captivity.

continued next page

3

My men were clothed all in green,
And they did ever attend on thee.
All this was gallant to be seen,
And yet, thou wouldst not love me.
Thou couldst desire no earthly thing,
But soon thou hadst it readily.
Thy music still I play and sing,
And yet thou wilt not love me.

4

Well, I shall petition God on high,
That thou my constancy mayest see,
And that yet once before I die,
That thou wilt vouchsafe to love me.
Ah, Greensleeves, farewell, adieu,
And God, I trust, shall prosper thee.
For I am still thy lover true.
Come back once more and love me.

5

Ye watchful guardians of the fair,
Who skim on wings of ambient air,
Of my dear Delia take a care,
And represent her lover
With all the gaiety of youth,
With honor, justice, love, and truth,
Till I return, her passions soothe.
For me in whispers move her.

6

Be careful no base sordid slave
With soul sunk in a golden grave
Who knows no virtue but to save
With glaring gold bewitch her.
Tell her for me she was designed—
For me, who knows how to be kind,
And have more plenty in my mind
Than one who's ten times richer.

7

Let all the world turn upside-down
And fools run an eternal round
In quest of what can ne'er be found,
To please their own ambitions.
Let little minds great charms espy
In shadows which at distance lie,
Whose hoped-for pleasure, when come nigh,
Proves nothing in fruition.

8

But cast into a mold divine,
Fair Delia does with luster shine.
Her virtuous soul's an ample mine
That yields a constant treasure.
Let poets in sublimest verse
Employ their skills, her fame rehearse,
Let sons of music pass whole days
With well-tuned flutes to please her.

My Darling Clementine

In a ca - vern, in a can - yon,

ex - ca - va___ - ting for a mine;

Dwelt a min - er, for - ty - nin - er

and his daugh - ter, Clem - en - tine.

Chorus: Oh, my dar - ling, oh, my dar - ling,

Oh, my dar___ - ling Clem - en - tine!

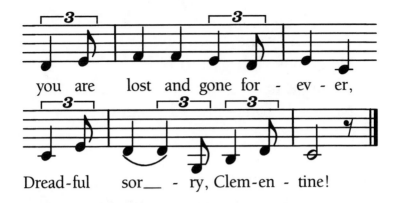

you are lost and gone for - ev - er,

Dread-ful sor__ - ry, Clem-en - tine!

2

Light she was, and like a fairy,
And her shoes were number nine.
Herring boxes without topses,
Sandals were for Clementine.

chorus

3

Drove she ducklings to the water
Every morning just at nine.
Struck her toe against a splinter,
Fell into the foaming brine.

chorus

4

Ruby lips above the water
Blowing bubbles soft and fine.
Woe is me, I was no swimmer,
So I lost my Clementine.

chorus

continued next page

19

Then the miner, Forty-Niner
He grew sad, began to pine,
Thought he oughter "jine" his daughter.
Now he's gone – like Clementine.

chorus

6

In a churchyard, near the canyon,
Where the myrtle shoots entwine
There grow rosies, 'n' other posies
Fertilized by Clementine.

chorus

7

In my dreams she still doth haunt me,
Robed in garments soaked in brine.
Though in life I used to hug her,
Now she's dead, I'll draw the line.

chorus

I've Been Working on the Railroad

I've been work-ing on the rail-road all the live-long day. I've been work-ing on the rail-road just to pass the time a - way. Don't you hear the whis-tle blow-ing? Rise up so ear - ly in the morn!

21

continued next page

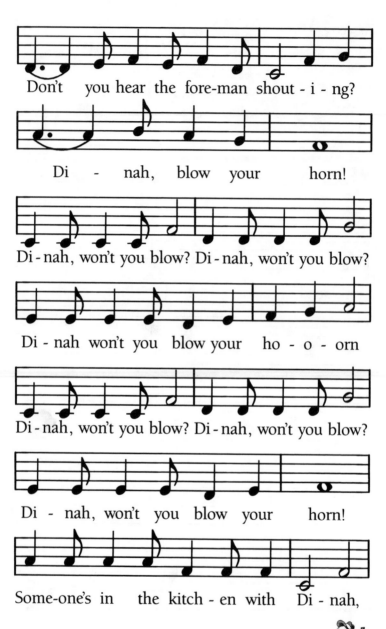

Don't you hear the fore-man shout-i-ng?

Di - nah, blow your horn!

Di-nah, won't you blow? Di-nah, won't you blow?

Di - nah won't you blow your ho - o - orn

Di-nah, won't you blow? Di-nah, won't you blow?

Di - nah, won't you blow your horn!

Some-one's in the kitch - en with Di - nah,

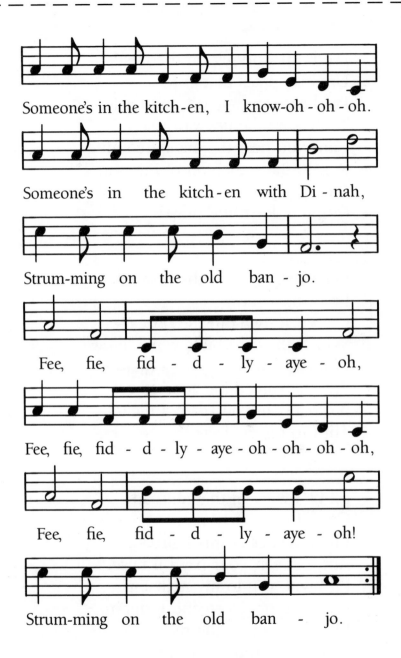

Someone's in the kitch-en, I know-oh - oh - oh.

Someone's in the kitch-en with Di - nah,

Strum-ming on the old ban - jo.

Fee, fie, fid - d - ly - aye - oh,

Fee, fie, fid - d - ly - aye - oh - oh - oh - oh,

Fee, fie, fid - d - ly - aye - oh!

Strum-ming on the old ban - jo.

continued next page

2

I've been working on the trestle,
Driving spikes that grip.
I've been working on the trestle,
To be sure the ties won't slip.
Can't you hear the engine coming?
Run to the stanchion of the bridge!
Can't you see the big black smokestack
Coming down the ridge?

chorus

3

I've been living in the boxcars.
I'm a hobo now.
I've been living in the boxcars,
Which the yard bulls won't allow.
Brother, can you spare a quarter?
Buy me something good to eat?
Brother, can you spare a nickel,
Till I'm on my feet?

chorus

4

I'll be owner of this railroad
One of these here days.
I'll be owner of this railroad,
And I swear, your pay I'll raise.
I'll invite you to my mansion,
Feed you on goose and terrapin.
I'll invite you to the racetrack
When my ship comes in.

chorus

When Johnny Comes Marching Home Again

When John - ny comes march-ing

home a - gain, Hur - rah____! Hur -

rah____! We'll give him a har-dy

wel - come then, Hur - rah____! Hur -

rah____! The men will cheer, the

boys will shout, The la - dies they will

continued next page

25

all   turn   out, And   we'll   all   feel

gay   when   John - ny   comes march - ing

home___. And we'll   all   feel   gay when

John - ny comes march-ing   home___.

2
The old churchbell will peal with joy
    Hurrah! Hurrah!
To welcome home our darling boy.
    Hurrah! Hurrah!
The village lads and lassies say
With roses they will strew the way.

           chorus

3
Get ready for the Jubilee.
    Hurrah! Hurrah!
We'll give the hero three times three.

Hurrah! Hurrah!
The laurel wreath is ready now
To place upon his loyal brow.

chorus

4

Let love and friendship on that day
Hurrah! Hurrah!
Their choicest treasures then display.
Hurrah! Hurrah!
And let each one perform some part
To fill with joy his warrior's heart.

chorus

America! (My Country, 'Tis of Thee)

My coun-try! 'Tis of thee,

Sweet land of lib - er - ty,

Of thee I sing.

Land where my fa - thers died,

Land of the pil - grims' pride

From ev - e - ry____ moun - tain - side

Let___ free - dom ring. (Repeats)

2

My native country! Thee,
Land of the noble free,
Thy name I love.
I love thy rocks and rills,
Thy woods and templed hills.
My heart with rapture thrills,
Like that above.

3

Let music swell the breeze
And sing from all the trees
Sweet freedom's song.
Let mortal tongues awake,
Let all that breathe partake,
Let rocks their silence break,
The sound prolong.

4

Our father's God! To Thee,
Author of liberty,
To Thee we sing.
Long may our land be bright
With freedom's holy light.

continued next page

Protect us by Thy might,
Great God our king.

5

God bless our native land.
Firm may she ever stand,
Through storm and night.
When the wild tempests rave,
Ruler of wind and wave,
Do Thou our country save,
By Thy great might.

6

For her our prayer shall rise
To God above the skies.
On Him we wait.
Thou, who are ever nigh,
Guarding with watchful eye,
To Thee aloud we cry,
"God save the state!"

7

Lord of all truth and right,
In Whom alone is might
On Thee we call.
Give us prosperity,
Give us true liberty.
May all th' oppressed go free.
God save us all!

I Wish I Were in Dixie (Dixie Land)

I___ wish I were___ in the

land of cot - ton. Old times there are

not for - got-ten. Look a - way! Look a -

way! Look a - way! Dix - ie Land. In___

Dix - ie Land___ where___ I was born in,

Ear - ly on one fros - ty morn-in'. Look a -

31

continued next page

way! Look a-way! Look a - way! Dix-ie Land.

Chorus: Then I wish I was in Dix-ie___. Hoo -

ray! Hoo - ray! In Dix - ie Land I'll

take my stand, To live and die in

Dix - ie____. A - way, a - way, a -

way down south in Dix - ie____, A - way,

a - way, a - way down south in Dix - ie__.

2

Old Missus married Will the Weaver.
William was a gay deceiver.
Look away! Look away! Look away!
    Dixie Land.
But when he put his arm around her,
He smiled as fierce as a forty-pounder.
Look away! Look away! Look away!
    Dixie Land.

chorus

3

His face was sharp as a butcher's cleaver,
But that did not seem to grieve her.
Look away! Look away! Look away!
    Dixie Land.
Old Missus acted the foolish part
And died for a man that broke her heart.
Look away! Look away! Look away!
    Dixie Land.

chorus

4

Now here's a toast to the next old Missus,
And all the girls that want to kiss us.
Look away! Look away! Look away!
    Dixie Land.
But if you want to drive 'way sorrow,
Come and hear this song tomorrow.

continued next page

Look away! Look away! Look away!
   Dixie Land.

chorus

5

There's buckwheat cakes and Injun batter,
Makes you fat or a little fatter.
Look away! Look away! Look away!
   Dixie Land.
Then hoe it down and scratch your gravel.
To Dixie Land I'm bound to travel.
Look away! Look away! Look away!
   Dixie Land.

chorus

6

Gonna cook a meal of grits and 'taters,
Feed what's left to the alligators.
Look away! Look away! Look away!
   Dixie Land.
And when I die, see that they lay me
'Neath an oak that's cool and shady.
Look away! Look away! Look away!
   Dixie Land.

chorus

Shenandoah

Oh, Shen - an - doah, I love your daugh - ter__. A____ - way__, you roll - ing riv - er__. I'll take her cross yon__ - der wa - ter__.

Chorus: A____ - way__, we're bound a - way. 'Cross the wide__ Mis - sou__ - ri.

continued next page

2

Oh, Shenandoah, she took my fancy.
Away, you rolling river.
Oh, Shenandoah, I love your Nancy.

chorus

3

Oh, Shenandoah, I long to see you.
Away, you rolling river.
Oh, Shenandoah, I'm drawing near you.

chorus

4

Oh, Shenandoah, I'm bound to leave you.
Away, you rolling river.
Oh, Shenandoah, I'll ne'er deceive you.

chorus

5

Oh, Shenandoah, I'll ne'er forget you.
Away, you rolling river.
Oh, Shenandoah, I'll ever love you.

chorus

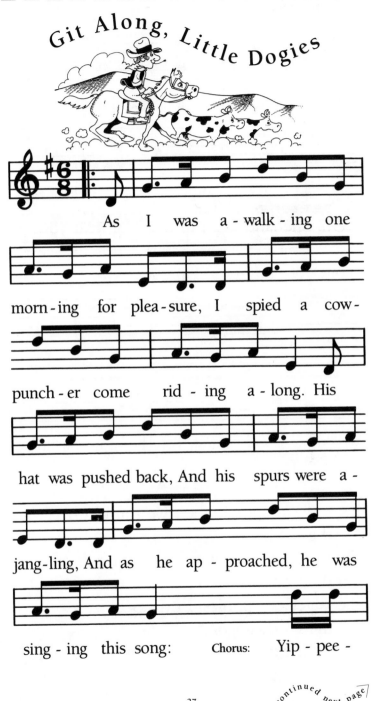

Git Along, Little Dogies

As I was a - walk - ing one morn - ing for plea - sure, I spied a cow - punch - er come rid - ing a - long. His hat was pushed back, And his spurs were a - jang - ling, And as he ap - proached, he was sing - ing this song: **Chorus:** Yip - pee -

continued next page

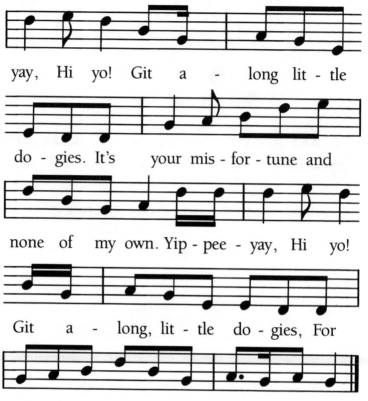

yay, Hi yo! Git a - long lit - tle

do - gies. It's your mis - for - tune and

none of my own. Yip - pee - yay, Hi yo!

Git a - long, lit - tle do - gies, For

you know Wy - o - ming 'll be your new home.

2

It's early in spring when we round up
    the dogies,
We rope 'em and brand 'em and bob off
    their tails,
We water our ponies, load up
    the chuckwagon,
And then drive the dogies out onto the trail.

chorus

3

Some boys, they go out on the trail just
for pleasure,
But that's where they get it most
terribly wrong—
You'd never imagine the trouble they give us!
It takes all we've got to keep moving along.

chorus

4

It's yelling and whooping and driving
the dogies,
And oh, how we wish they would kindly
move on.
It's whooping and punching and Git on,
little dogies,
For you know Wyoming must be your
new home.

chorus

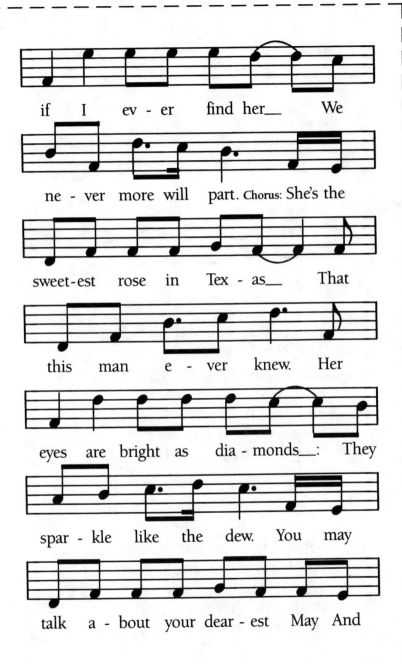

if I ev - er find her___ We

ne - ver more will part. Chorus: She's the

sweet-est rose in Tex - as___ That

this man e - ver knew. Her

eyes are bright as dia - monds___: They

spar - kle like the dew. You may

talk a - bout your dear - est May And

41

continued next page

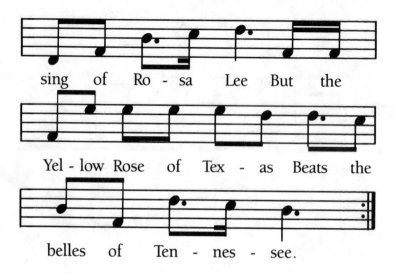

sing of Ro - sa Lee But the

Yel - low Rose of Tex - as Beats the

belles of Ten - nes - see.

2

Where the Rio Grande is flowing
And starry skies are bright,
She walks along the river
In the quiet summer night.
She asks if I remember
When we parted long ago.
I promised to come back again,
And not to leave her so.

chorus

3

Oh, now I'm going to find her
For my heart is full of woe.
We'll sing the songs together
We sung so long ago.
We'll play the banjo gaily,
We'll sing the songs of yore,
And the Yellow Rose of Texas
Will be mine forevermore.

chorus

Goober Peas

Sit - ting   by   the   road - side

On   a   sum - mer's   day,   Chat - ting

with   my   mess-mates   Pass - ing   time   a -

way,   Ly - ing   in   the   shad - ows,

un - der - neath the   trees   Good - ness,

how de - li - cious   Eat - ing goo - ber

continued next page

peas! Chorus: Peas, peas, peas, peas!

Eat - ing goo - ber peas!

Good-ness, how de - li - cious,

Eat - ing goo - ber peas! (Repeats)

2

When a horseman rides by,
The soldiers have a rule
To cry out at their loudest,
"Mister, here's your mule!"
But another pleasure enchantinger
    than these
Is wearing out your grinders
Eating goober peas!

chorus

3

Just before the battle
The General hears a row.
He says, "The Yanks are coming,
I hear their rifles now!"
He turns around in wonder, and
    what d'you think he sees?
The Georgia Militia
Eating goober peas!

                    chorus

4

I think this song has lasted
Almost long enough.
The subject's interesting,
But rhyming's mighty rough.
I wish this war was over when,
    free from rags and fleas,
We'll kiss our wives and
    sweethearts
And gobble goober peas.

                    chorus

The Erie Canal

I've got a mule, her name is Sal____. Fif - teen miles on the E - rie Ca - nal____. She's a good old work - er and a good old pal____. Fif - teen miles on the E - rie Ca - nal____. We've hauled some

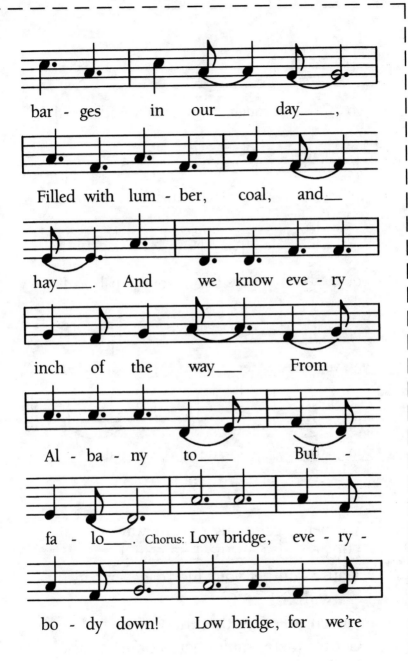

bar - ges   in   our____   day____,

Filled with lum - ber,   coal,   and__

hay____.   And   we know eve - ry

inch   of   the   way____   From

Al - ba - ny   to____   Buf__ -

fa - lo____. Chorus: Low bridge,   eve - ry -

bo - dy down!   Low bridge, for we're

continued next page

go - ing through a town. And you'll

al - ways know your neigh - bor, And

you'll al - ways know your pal, If

you've ev - er nav - i - gat - ed

on the E - rie Ca - nal___.

2

We better get along on our way, old gal.
Fifteen miles on the Erie Canal.
'Cause you bet your life I'd never part
    with Sal.
Fifteen miles on the Erie Canal.
Get up there, mule, here comes a lock.
We'll make Rome 'bout six o'clock.

One more trip and back we'll go,
Right back home to Buffalo.

chorus

3

Now where would I be if I lost my pal?
Fifteen miles on the Erie Canal.
I'd like to see a mule half as good as Sal.
Fifteen miles on the Erie Canal.
A fool barge-cap'n once got her sore.
Now he's got a broken jaw,
'Cause she let fly with her iron shoe,
And knocked him clear to Timbuctoo.

chorus

4

You can hear them sing all about
    my gal.
Fifteen miles on the Erie Canal.
It's a right fine ditty 'bout my mule Sal.
Fifteen miles on the Erie Canal.
Every band will be playin' it soon—
Darn fool words and a darn fool tune,
But you'd better learn it before you go
On board the barge at Buffalo.

chorus

Funiculi, Funicula

Some think the world is made for fun and fro - lic And so do I! And so do I! Some think It well to be all mel - an - chol - ic, To pine and sigh, To pine and

sigh. But I, I love

to spend my time in sing - ing

Some joy - ous song, Some

joy - ous song. To set

the air with mu - sic brave - ly

ring - ing Is far from wrong,

Is far from wrong___!

continued next page

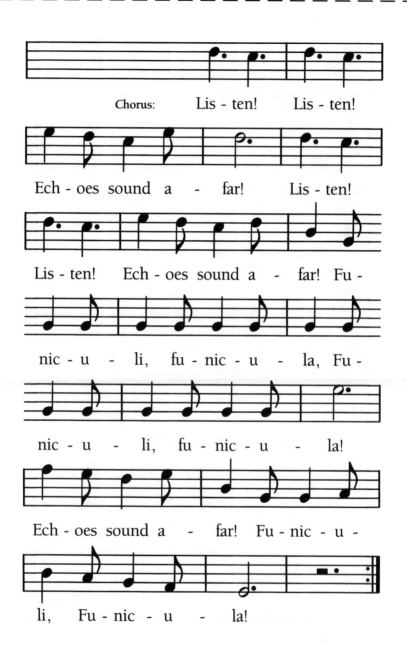

Chorus: Lis - ten! Lis - ten!

Ech - oes sound a - far! Lis - ten!

Lis - ten! Ech - oes sound a - far! Fu -

nic - u - li, fu - nic - u - la, Fu -

nic - u - li, fu - nic - u - la!

Ech - oes sound a - far! Fu - nic - u -

li, Fu - nic - u - la!

2

Some think it wrong to set the
    feet a-dancing!
But not so I!
But not so I!
Some think that eyes should keep
    from coyly glancing
Upon the sly,
Upon the sly.
But oh, to me the mazy dance
    is charming,
Divinely sweet,
Divinely sweet!
For surely there is nought that
    is alarming
In nimble feet,
In nimble feet!

chorus

3

Ah, me! 'Tis strange that some
    should take to sighing,
And like it well,
And like it well!
For me, I have not thought it
    worth the trying,
So cannot tell,

continued next page

So cannot tell!
With laugh and dance and song
    the day soon passes,
Full soon is gone,
Full soon is gone!
For mirth was made for joyous
    lads and lasses
To call their own,
To call their own!

chorus

The Streets of Laredo

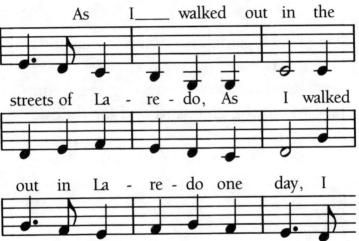

As I___ walked out in the

streets of La - re - do, As I walked

out in La - re - do one day, I

spied a poor cow - boy wrapped up in

white lin - en, Wrapped up in white

lin - en and cold as the clay.

continued next page

55

2

"I see by your outfit that you are a cowboy."
These words he did say as I boldly
        stepped by.
"Come sit down beside me and hear
        my sad story—
I was shot in the chest and I know
        I must die.

3

"Let sixteen gamblers come serve as my
        mourners.
Let sixteen cowboys come sing me a song.
Take me to the graveyard and lay the sod
        o'er me,
For I'm a poor cowboy and I know I've
        done wrong.

4

"It was once in the saddle I used
        to go dashing.
It was once in the saddle I'd ride all the day.
'Twas first to drinking and then to
        card playing,
Got shot in the chest, and I'm dying today.

5

"Get six jolly cowboys to carry my coffin.
Get six pretty maids to carry my pall.
Put bunches of roses all over my coffin,
White roses to soften the clods as they fall.

6

"Oh, beat the drum slowly and play the
        fife lowly
And play a sad dirge as you tote me along.
Take me to the valley and lay the earth
        o'er me,
For I'm a young cowpoke and I know I've
        done wrong."

7

We beat the drum slowly and played the
        fife lowly,
And bitterly wept as we bore him along.
For we all loved our comrade, so brave and
        so handsome,
We all loved our cowboy although he'd
        done wrong.

Sweet Betsy From Pike

Have you heard the tale of Sweet

Bet - sy from Pike, Who crossed the high

Rock-ies with her lov - er Ike, With

two yoke of cat - tle, and one yal - ler

dog, A tall Shang-hai roos - ter, and

one spot - ted hog? Chorus: Say - ing,

"Love you, Pike Coun - ty, Fare - well just the same We'll be back a - gain When we've panned out our claim."

Alternate chorus:

Sighing, "Goodbye, Pike County,
Farewell for a while.
We'll see you again
When we've panned out our pile."

2

One evening quite early, they camped
    by the Platte.
'Twas close by the road on a green
    shady flat
Where Betsy, quite tired, lay down to
    repose
While loving Ike gazed on his Pike
    County rose,

continued next page

3

Came some Injuns on horseback, a wild
yelling horde.
And they terrified Betsy, who prayed to
the Lord.
Beneath their big wagon the couple did
crawl
And drove off the Injuns with musket
and ball.

chorus

4

They trudged the deep valleys and crossed
the tall peaks,
And lived off of berries and water for weeks,
And nearly got drowned in a fast mountain
stream,
For to reach California was their only
dream.

alternate chorus

5

The rooster ran off and the cattle all died.
Their last strip of bacon that morning
they fried.
Poor Ike was discouraged, and Betsy
was mad.
The dog wagged his tail and looked
wonderfully sad.

chorus

6

They soon hit the desert, where Betsy
    gave out,
And in the hot sands she lay, rolling about,
While Ike cried hot tears, looking on in
    surprise,
And said, "Betsy, get up–you'll get sand in
    your eyes."

alternate chorus

7

Sweet Betsy rose up in considerable pain,
And said she'd return to Pike County again,
But Ike shook his head, and they fondly
    embraced,
And onward she traveled, his arm 'round
    her waist,

chorus

8

One morning they climbed up a very
    high hill,
And with wonder looked down into old
    Placerville.
Ike shouted and said, as his eyes down
    he cast,
"Sweet Betsy, my darling, we've made
    it at last."

alternate chorus

continued next page

9

Long Ike and sweet Betsy attended a dance,
Where Ike wore a pair of his Pike
County pants.
Sweet Betsy was all dressed up in ribbons
and rings.
Said Ike, "You're an angel, but where are
your wings?"

chorus

10

A miner asked, "Betsy, will you dance
with me?"
"I will," she replied, "if you don't make
too free,
And don't dance me too hard.
Do you want to know why?
Doggone you, I'm brim-full of strong alkali."

alternate chorus

11

Long Ike and sweet Betsy got married in May.
And dwelled in a shack in the hills,
so they say.
After six months in 'Frisco, Long Ike
met a girl—
A sweet-looking dancer who gave him a
whirl.

chorus

12

Ike spoke of poor Betsy as "just an
old horse."
What was Betsy to do? She gave Ike a
divorce.
Once more a free woman, she said
with a shout,
"Goodbye, you big lummox, it's time you
cleared out."

alternate chorus

13

Well, Betsy went back to Pike County
that May,
And Ike lost his dancer and soon
passed away.
If this story's too sad, you can cry if you like
For that mighty fine woman, sweet Betsy
of Pike.

chorus

Yankee Doodle

Fa - ther and I went

down to camp A - long with Cap - tain

Good - win And there we saw the

men and boys As thick as has - ty

pud-ding. Chorus: Yan - kee Doo - dle,

keep it up! Yan - kee Doo - dle

Dan - dy, Mind the mu - sic and the step, And with the girls be han - dy.

2

And there we saw a thousand men,
As rich as Squire David
And what they wasted every day,
I wish it could be savèd.

chorus

3

And there was Captain Washington
Upon a strapping stallion
A-giving orders to his men—
I guess there was a million.

chorus

4

And then the feathers on his hat,
They looked so very fine, ah!
I wanted one of them to get,
To give to my Jemimah.

chorus

5

And there I saw a swamping gun,
Large as a log of maple,
Upon a mighty little cart,
A load for father's cattle.

chorus

6

And every time they fired it off,
It took a horn of powder.
It made a noise like father's gun,
Except a whole lot louder.

chorus

7

And there I saw a little drum,
Its heads all made of leather.
They knocked upon't with
    little sticks
To call the troops together.

chorus

8

And Captain Davis had a gun,
He clapped his hand upon it,
And stuck a crooked stabbing iron
Upon the little end on't.

chorus

9

And Uncle Sam came there to charge
Some pancakes and some onions
And 'lasses cakes to carry home
To give his wife and young ones.

chorus

10

And there they'd fife away for fun
And play on cornstalk fiddles
And some wore ribbons red as blood
Bound tight around their middles.

chorus

11

The troopers, too, would gallop up
And shoot right in our faces.
It scared me almost half to death
To see them run such races.

chorus

12

It scared me so that I ran off,
Nor stopped, as I remember,
Nor turned about till I got home,
Locked up in mother's chamber.

chorus

On Top of Old Smoky

Chorus: On top of old Smo -
ky____, All co-vered with snow____,
I lost my true lo - ver____
From a - court-in' too slow____.

1

On top of old Smoky
I went for to weep,
For a false-hearted lover
Is worse than a thief.

chorus optional

2

For a thief, he will rob you
Of all that you have,
But a false-hearted lover
Will send you to your grave.

chorus optional

3

He'll hug you and kiss you
And tell you more lies
Than the ties of the railroad
Or the stars in the skies.

Hush, Little Baby

Hush, lit-tle ba-by, don't say a

word, Dad-dy's gon-na buy you a

mock-ing bird. And if that mock-

ing bird don't sing, Dad-dy's gon-na

buy you a dia-mond ring. **(Repeats)**

2

If that diamond ring is brass,
Daddy's gonna buy you a looking glass.
If that looking glass gets broke,
Daddy's gonna buy you a nanny goat.

3

If that goat don't give no milk,
Daddy's gonna buy you a robe of silk.
If that robe of silk gets worn,
Daddy's gonna buy you a big French horn.

4

If that big French horn won' play,
Daddy's gonna buy you a candy cane.
If that cane should lose its stripes,
Daddy's gonna buy you a set of pipes.

5

If that set of pipes ain' clean,
Daddy's gonna buy you a jumping bean.
If that jumping bean won' roll,
Daddy's gonna buy you a lump of coal.

continued next page

6

If that lump of coal won' burn,
Daddy's gonna buy you a butter churn.
If that butter turns out sour,
Daddy's gonna buy you an orchid flower.

7

If that flower don' smell sweet,
Daddy's gonna buy you some salted
    meat.
If that salted meat won' fry,
Daddy's gonna buy you an apple pie.

8

When that apple pie's all done,
Daddy's gonna buy you another one.
When that pie's all eaten up,
Daddy's gonna buy you a greyhound pup.

9

If that dog won' run the course,
Daddy's gonna buy you a rocking horse.
If that rocking horse won' rock,
Daddy's gonna buy you a cuckoo clock.

10

And if that cuckoo clock runs down,
You're still the prettiest little girl in town.

Home on the Range

Oh, give me a home where the buf - fa - lo roam, Where the deer and the an - te - lope play, Where sel - dom is heard a dis - cour - ag - ing word, and the sky is not clou - ded all day____.

Chorus: Home, home on the range____!

73

continued next page

Where the deer and the an - te - lope play____, Where sel - dom is heard A dis - cour - a - ging word, And the sky is not cloud - ed all day____.

2

Oh, give me a gale on some soft
    Southern vale,
Where the stream of life joyfully flows,
On the banks of the river, where
    seldom if ever,
Any poisonous herbiage grows.

chorus

3

Oh, give me a land where the bright
    diamond sands
Lie awash in the glittering stream,

Where days glide along in leisure
and song,
And afternoons pass as a dream.

chorus

4

I love the bright flowers in this frontier
of ours,
And I thrill to the eagle's shrill scream.
Blood red are the rocks, brown the
antelope flocks
That browse on the prairie so green.

chorus

5

The breezes are pure, and the sky
is azure,
And the zephyrs so balmy and slow,
That I would not exchange my home on
the range
For a townhouse in San Francisco.

chorus

6

How often at night, when the heavens
are bright
With the light of the unclouded stars,
Have I stood here amazed and asked, as
I gazed
If their glory exceeds that of ours.

chorus

The John B. Sails (The Sloop John B.)

Oh, we came on the sloop *John* B., My grand-fa-ther and me. 'Round Nas-sau Town____ we____ did roam.

Drink-ing all night, we got in____ - to a fight.

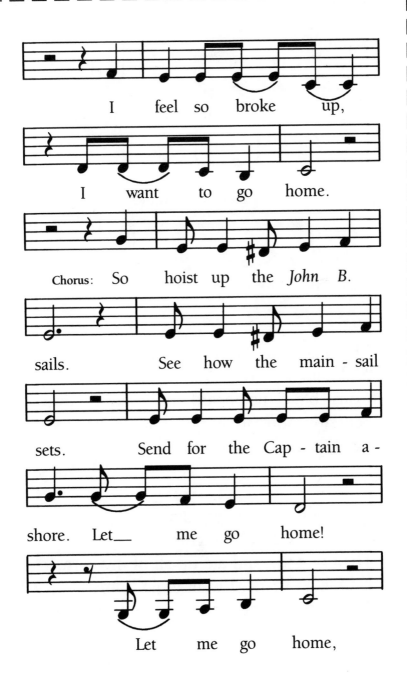

I feel so broke up,

I want to go home.

Chorus: So hoist up the *John B.*

sails. See how the main - sail

sets. Send for the Cap - tain a -

shore. Let___ me go home!

Let me go home,

77

continued next page

Let__ me go home.

I feel so broke up,

I want to go home.

2

The first mate, he got drunk,
Broke up somebody's trunk.
Constable came aboard and took him away.
Sergeant John Stone, please leave me alone.
I feel so broke up, I want to go home.

chorus

3

The poor cook, he got fits,
Threw 'way all of the grits,
Then he took and ate up all of my corn.
Let me go home, I want to go home.
This is the worst trip since I've been born.

Little Brown Jug

My wife and I lived all a-
lone, In a lit-tle log hut we
called our own. She loved gin, and
I loved rum. I tell you what, we'd
lots of fun! **Chorus:** Ha, ha, ha,
you and me, Lit-tle brown jug, don't

79

continued next page

I love thee. Ha, ha, ha, you and me,

Lit - tle brown jug, don't I love thee.

2

'Tis you who makes my friends my foes
'Tis you who makes me wear old clothes,
Here you are, so near my nose,
So tip her up, and down she goes.

chorus

3

When I go toiling to my farm,
I take little brown jug under my arm.
I place it under a shady tree.
Little brown jug, 'tis you and me.

chorus

4

If all the folks in Adam's race
Were gathered together in one place,
Then I'd prepare to shed a tear
Before I'd part from you, my dear.

chorus

5

If I'd a cow that gave such milk,
I'd clothe her in the finest silk.
I'd feed her on the choicest hay,
And milk her forty times a day.

chorus

6

The rose is red; my nose is, too.
The violet's blue, and so
    are you.
And yet I guess before I stop,
We'd better take another drop.

chorus

The Happy Wanderer

I am a hap-py wan-der-er A - long the moun-tain track, And as I go, I love to sing, My knap-sack on my back.

Chorus: Val - de - ri, Val - de - rah, Val - de - ri, Val - de - rah— ha, ha, ha,

ha, ha, Val - de - ri, Val - de -
rah, My knap-sack on my back.

2

I love to wander by the stream
That dances in the sun.
So joyously it calls to me,
"Come join my happy song."

chorus

Come join my happy song.

3

I wave my hat to all I meet,
And they wave back to me.
And blackbirds call so loud and sweet
From every greenwood tree.

chorus

From every greenwood tree.

continued next page

4

Oh, may I go a-wandering
Until the day I die.
Oh, may I always laugh and sing
Beneath God's clear blue sky.

chorus

Beneath God's clear blue sky.

Michael, Row the Boat Ashore

Chorus: Mich-ael, row the boat a - shore___. Al - le - lu - ia! Mich - ael, row the boat a - shore. Al - le - lu - u - ia!

1

The River Jordan is chilly and cold.
Allelu-ia!
Chills the body, but not the soul.
Allelu-u-ia!

chorus

85

continued next page

2

River is deep, and the river is wide.
Allelu-ia!
Milk and honey on the other side.
Allelu-u-ia!

chorus

3

Brother, help me trim the sail.
Allelu-ia!
If we've faith, we cannot fail.
Allelu-u-ia!

chorus

4

River is quick, and the river is fast.
Allelu-ia!
But we shall reach that shore at last.
Allelu-u-ia!

chorus

5

Skies are black, and the wind's northwest.
Allelu-ia!
Grip that tiller and do your best.
Allelu-u-ia!

chorus

6

Sister, help him lock the oar.
Allelu-ia!
And he'll row the boat ashore.
Allelu-u-ia!

chorus

She'll Be Comin' 'Round the Mountain

She'll be com - in' 'round the

moun - tain When she comes.

She'll be com - in' 'round the moun-tain

When she comes. She'll be

com - in' 'round the moun-tain. She'll be

com - in' 'round the moun-tain. She'll be

87

continued next page

com - in' 'round the moun-tain When she comes.

2

She'll be driving six white horses
When she comes.

repeat, as in first verse

3

She'll be shining bright as silver
When she comes.

repeat, as in first verse

4

She will neither rock nor totter
When she comes.

repeat, as in first verse

5

Oh, we'll all go out to meet her
When she comes.

repeat, as in first verse

6

We will kill the old red rooster
When she comes.

repeat, as in first verse

7

And we'll all have chicken and
dumplings

When she comes.

repeat, as in first verse

8

There'll be joy and smiles and
laughter
When she comes.

repeat, as in first verse

9

She will drive us all to Heaven
When she comes.

repeat, as in first verse

Swanee River (Old Folks at Home)

Way down up - on the
Swa - nee Riv - er Far, far a -
way, That's where my heart is
turn - ing ev - er, There's where the
old folks stay. All up and
down the whole cre - a - tion Sad -

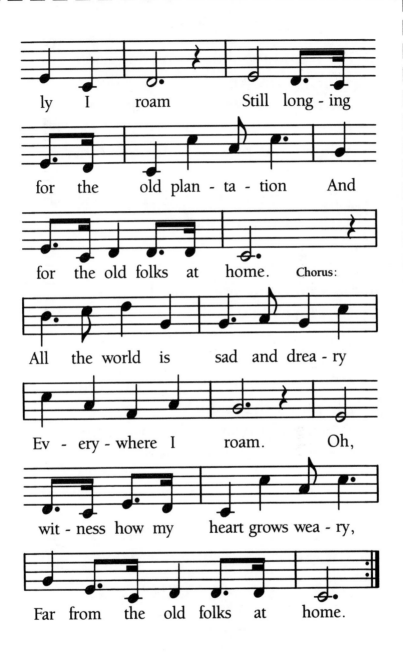

ly I roam Still long - ing

for the old plan - ta - tion And

for the old folks at home. Chorus:

All the world is sad and drea - ry

Ev - ery - where I roam. Oh,

wit - ness how my heart grows wea - ry,

Far from the old folks at home.

91

continued next page

2

All 'round the little farm I wandered
When I was young.
Then, many happy days I squandered,
Many the songs I sung.
When I was playing with my brother,
Happy was I.
Oh, take me to my kind old mother,
There let me live and die.

chorus

3

One little hut among the bushes,
One that I love,
Still sadly to my memory rushes
No matter where I rove.
When will I see the bees a-humming
All 'round the comb?
When will I hear the banjo strumming
Down in my dear old home?

chorus

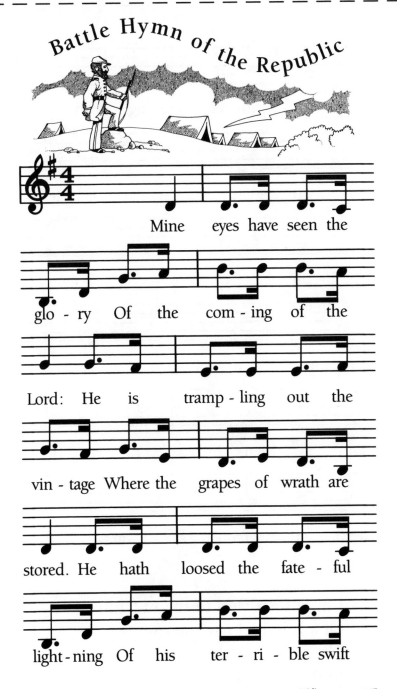

Battle Hymn of the Republic

Mine eyes have seen the glo - ry Of the com - ing of the Lord: He is tramp - ling out the vin - tage Where the grapes of wrath are stored. He hath loosed the fate - ful light - ning Of his ter - ri - ble swift

continued next page

93

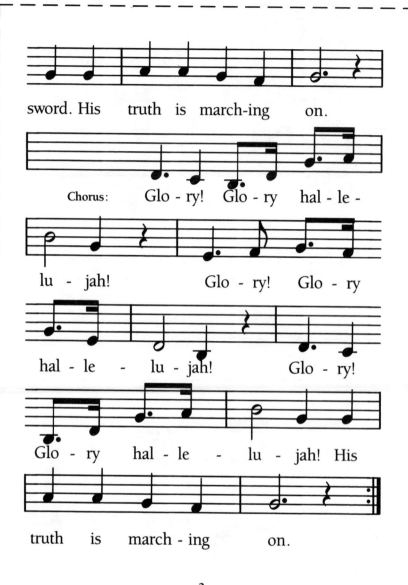

sword. His truth is march-ing on.

Chorus: Glo - ry! Glo - ry hal - le -

lu - jah! Glo - ry! Glo - ry

hal - le - lu - jah! Glo - ry!

Glo - ry hal - le - lu - jah! His

truth is march - ing on.

2

I have seen Him in the watchfires
Of a hundred circling camps.
They have builded Him an altar
In the evening dews and damps.

94

I can read His righteous sentence
By the dim and flaring lamps.
His day is marching on.

chorus

3

I have read a fiery gospel
Writ in burnished rows of steel:
"As ye deal with my condemnors,
So with ye my grace shall deal."
Let the hero born of woman
Crush the serpent with his heel,
Since God is marching on.

chorus

4

He has sounded forth the trumpet
That shall never call retreat.
He is sifting out the hearts of men
Before His judgment seat.
Oh be swift, my soul, to answer Him!
Be jubilant, my feet!
Our God is marching on.

chorus

5

In the beauty of the lilies
Christ was born across the sea,
With a glory in His bosom
That transfigures you and me.
As He died to make men holy
Let us die to make men free,
While God is marching on.

chorus

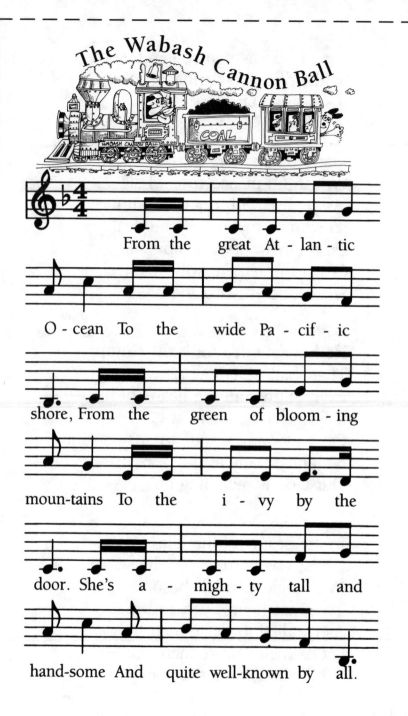

The Wabash Cannon Ball

From the great At - lan - tic O - cean To the wide Pa - cif - ic shore, From the green of bloom - ing moun - tains To the i - vy by the door. She's a - migh - ty tall and hand-some And quite well-known by all.

She's the mod - ern com - bi - na - tion—

Chorus: —On the Wa - bash Can - non Ball!

2

She came down from Birmingham
One cold December day.
As she rolled into the station,
You could hear the people say,
"There's a girl from Tennessee.
She's long and she is tall.
She came down from Memphis—

chorus

3

Now the eastern states are dandy,
So the western people say.
From New York to St. Louis,
And Chicago on the way,
From the hills of Minnesota
Where the rippling waters fall,
No chances can be taken—

chorus

continued next page

4

Will you listen to the whistle
And the rumble and the roar,
As she glides along the woodland,
Through the hills and by the shore.
Hear the throb of her great engine,
Hear the lonesome hobos squall,
"You're traveling through the jungle —

chorus

5

Here's to Daddy Klaxton!
May his name forever stand,
And always be remembered
Round the courts of our great land.
When his earthly race is over
And the curtains round him fall,
We shall carry him to glory

chorus

Kookaburra

Koo - ka - bur - ra   sits   in   the

old gum tree - ee.   Mer - ry, mer - ry

king   of   the   bush   is   he - ee.

Laugh, Koo - ka - bur - ra,   laugh, Koo - ka -

bur - ra,   Gay your life must   be.

continued next page

2

Kookaburra, sits in an old gum tree-ee,
Eating all the gumdrops he can see-ee.
Stop, Kookaburra, stop, Kookaburra,
Leave a few for me.

Jeanie with the Light Brown Hair

I dream of Jean - ie with the light brown___ hair Borne like a va - por on the gold - en air. I see her trip - ping where the bright streams___ play, Gay___ as the flow - ers a_____ - long her way.

continued next page

Chorus: Ma - ny are the fond

notes her mer - ry voice would pour,

Ech - oed by the birds in the

grove o'er and o'er. Ah! I dream

of Jean - ie with the light brown

hair, A_____ - float like va - por

on the soft sum - mer air.

2

I long for Jeanie with the day-dawn smile,
Radiant with gladness, warm with
    winning guile.
I hear her melodies attuned to love,
Warm as the sunlight lighting heav'n above.

chorus

3

I sigh for Jeanie when the daylight fades,
Hour when the shadow haunts the
    dewy glades,
And when the stars adorn the
    midnight skies,
I view their light as her own dear eyes.

chorus

4

Sighing like the night wind, and sobbing
    like the rain,
Waiting for my lost one who comes
    not again,
How I long for Jeanie, with my heart
    bowed low,
Never more to find her where the bright
    waters flow.

chorus

Camptown Races (Going to Run All Night)

The Camp-town la - dies

sing this song: Doo - dah! Doo - dah!

Camp - town race - track's five miles long.

Oh! Doo - dah day! I came down

there with my hat caved in. Doo - dah!

Doo - dah! I went back home with a

pock-et full of tin. Oh! Doo - dah day!

Chorus: Go - ing to run all night!

Go - ing to run all day! I'll

bet my mo - ney on the bob - tail nag–

Some - bo - dy bet on the bay.

2

The long-tail filly and the big black horse–
    Doo-dah! Doo-dah!
They fly the track and they both cut across.
    Oh! Doo-dah day!
The blind horse wallowed in a big
    mud hole–
    Doo-dah! Doo-dah!

continued next page

Can't touch bottom with a ten-foot pole.
  Oh! Doo-dah day!

chorus

3

Old muley cow came onto the track—
  Doo-dah! Doo-dah!
The bobtail flung her over his back.
  Oh! Doo-dah day!
Then flew along like a railroad car—
  Doo-dah! Doo-dah!
Running a race with a shooting star.
  Oh! Doo-dah day!

chorus

4

See them flying on a ten-mile heat—
  Doo-dah! Doo-dah!
'Round the racetrack, then repeat.
  Oh! Doo-dah day!
I won my money on the bobtail nag.
  Doo-dah! Doo-dah!
I keep my money in an old tow-bag.
  Oh! Doo-dah day!

chorus

Blow the Man Down

As____ I was a - walk - in' down

Par - a - dise Street, Sing - ing way, hay,

blow the man down, A sau - cy young

mai - den I chanced for to meet.

Give me some time to blow the man down.

107

continued next page

2

I asked, "Where're you bound?" She said,
    "Nowhere today,"
Singing way, hay, blow the man down,
"Now that's fine," I replied, "for I'm headed
    that way."
Give me some time to blow the man down.

3

We entered an ale-house looked down on
    the sea,
Singing way, hay, blow the man down,
There stood a policeman who stared right
    at me.
Give me some time to blow the man down.

4

Said he, "You're a pirate that flies the
    black flag,
Singing way, hay, blow the man down,
You've robbed some poor Dutchmen and left
    them in rags."
Give me some time to blow the man down.

5

"Oh, Officer, Officer, you do me wrong,
Singing way, hay, blow the man down,
I'm a freshwater sailor just in from
    Hong Kong."
Give me some time to blow the man down.

6

But they jailed me six months in Old
    Lexington Town,
Singing way, hay, blow the man down,
For fighting and kicking and knocking
    him down.
Give me some time to blow the man down.

7

Come all you brave sailors who follow
    the sea,
Singing way, hay, blow the man down,
And join in a-singing this chanty with me!
Give me some time to blow the man down!

'Round Her Neck She Wears a Yeller Ribbon

'Round her neck she wears a yel-ler rib-bon. She wears it in the spring____-time and in the month of May And if you ask her, "Why the dec-o-ra-tion?" She'll say, it's for her lov-er—Who is

fur, fur a - way! Fur a - way!

Fur a - way! She wears it for her

lov - er, who is fur, fur a - way.

2

'Round the park she walks a little baby.
She walks him in the winter
And the summer, so they say.
And if you ask her why on earth she
    walks him,
She walks him for her lover—
Who is fur, fur away!
Fur away! Fur away!
She walks him for her lover, who is fur,
    fur away.

3

That boy, he is a cunning little feller.
His birthday was a year ago,
Late in the month of May.

continued next page

And if you ask him, "Sonny, who's
    your daddy?"
He'll say, "My dad's a cowboy–
Who is fur, fur away!
Fur away! Fur away!
He'll say, "My dad's a cowboy who is fur,
    fur away."

4

Behind the door, her father keeps a shotgun.
It's loaded with a double dose
Of buckshot, so they say.
And if you ask him, "Why the ammunition?"
He keeps it for that cowboy–
Who is fur, fur away!
Fur away! Fur away!
He keeps it for that cowboy, who is fur,
    fur away.

5

Now on a grave she lays a wreath of flowers.
She lays it there in wintertime
And in the month of May.
And if you ask her who the wreath's to
    honor,
She'll say, "It's for my lover–Who has gone
    fur away."
Fur away! Fur away!
She'll say, "It's fer my cowboy who has gone
    fur away."

112

John Brown's Body

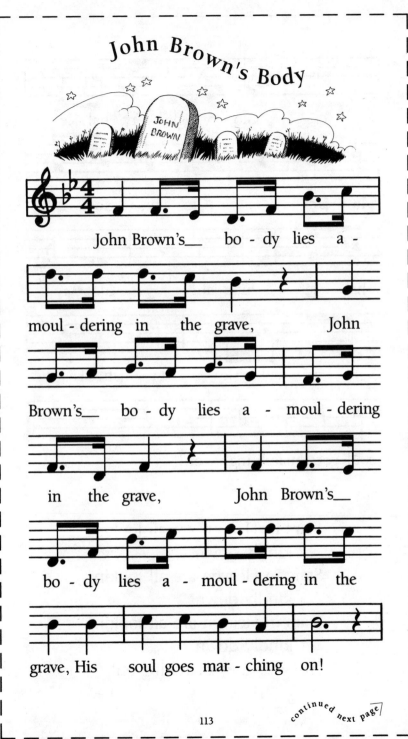

John Brown's__ bo - dy lies a -
moul - dering in the grave, John
Brown's__ bo - dy lies a - moul - dering
in the grave, John Brown's__
bo - dy lies a - moul - dering in the
grave, His soul goes mar - ching on!

continued next page

Chorus: Glo - ry, glo - ry hal - le - lu - jah! Glo - ry, glo - ry hal - le - lu - jah! Glo - ry, glo - ry hal - le - lu - jah! His soul goes march-ing on!

2

Stars in Heaven are all looking
    kindly down,
Stars in Heaven are all looking
    kindly down,
Stars in Heaven are all looking
    kindly down,
His soul goes marching on!

chorus

3

John Brown's knapsack is strapped
    upon his back,
John Brown's knapsack is strapped
    upon his back,
John Brown's knapsack is strapped
    upon his back,
His soul goes marching on!

chorus

4

He's gone to be a soldier in the army
    of the Lord,
He's gone to be a soldier in the army
    of the Lord,
He's gone to be a soldier in the army
    of the Lord,
His soul goes marching on!

chorus

Oh, Susanna!

I____ came from Al - a - bam - a With my ban - jo on my knee. I'm____ gone to Lou - 'si - an - a My true love for to see. It____ rained all night the day I left. The wea - ther, it was dry. The

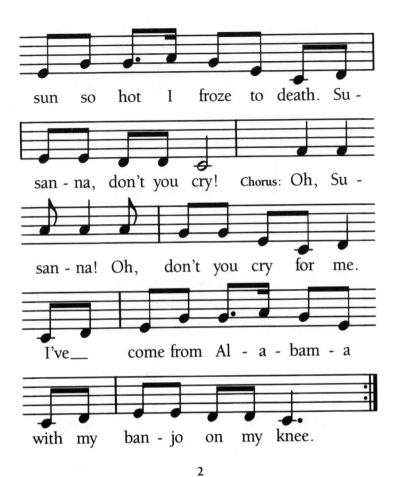

sun so hot I froze to death. Su -

san - na, don't you cry! Chorus: Oh, Su -

san - na! Oh, don't you cry for me.

I've__ come from Al - a - bam - a

with my ban - jo on my knee.

2

I jumped aboard the telegraph
And traveled down the wires.
The 'lectric fluid magnified
And lit five hundred fires.
The full moon burst, my horse ran off.
I really thought I'd die.
I shut my eyes to hold my breath.
Susanna, don't you cry!

chorus

continued next page

3

I had a dream the other night
When everything was still.
I thought I saw Susanna
A-coming down the hill.
A buckwheat cake was in her mouth
A tear was in her eye.
I said, "I'm coming from the South,
Susanna, don't you cry!"

chorus

4

I soon will be in New Orleans,
And then I'll look around,
And when I find Susanna,
I'll fall upon the ground.
But if I do not find my love,
Then surely I shall die.
But when I'm dead and six feet down,
Susanna, don't you cry!

chorus

The Caisson Song
(The Caissons Go Rolling Along)

O - ver hill, o - ver dale

We have hit the dus - ty trail,

And those cais - sons go roll - ing a -

long____! In and out, hear them

shout; Coun - ter - march and round a -

bout, While those cais - sons go roll - ing

119

continued next page

cais-sons are roll - ing a - long_____.

2

At the front, day and night,
Where the doughboys dig and fight—
And those caissons go rolling along!—
Our barrage will be there,
Adding to the rockets' glare,
While the caissons go rolling along.

chorus

3

Hear that whine? It's a shell!
Hit the dirt and dig like hell,
While the caissons go rolling along.
Comes the boom, stand up higher,
Take good aim, return the fire,
Help those caissons go rolling along!

chorus

4

Through the mud, through the lines,
Past the trenches and the mines,
Where the caissons go rolling along,
We won't rest till we see
Our brave lads taste victory,
And the caissons stop rolling along.

chorus

Meet Me in St. Louis, Louis

When Lou___ - is   came   to   the

flat_____,   He   hung   up   his

coat   and   his   hat_____.   He

gazed all   a - round, but   no   wi - fey

he   found, So   he   asked, "Where can

Flos - sie   be   at_____?"   A

note on the ta - ble he spied___.

He read it just once, then he

cried___. It ran, "Lou - is

dear, It's too slow for me here, So

I think I will go for a

ride___. **Chorus:** "Meet me in St.

Lou - is, Lou - is, Meet me at the

continued next page/

Fair___. Don't tell me that

lights are shin - ing A - ny place but

there__. We will dance the Hoot-chee

Koot - chie____, I will be your

toot - sie woot - sie, If you will

meet me in St. Lou - is, Lou - is,

Meet me at the Fair___."

2

The dresses that hung in the hall
Were gone – she had taken them all.
She took all his rings, and the rest of
  his things.
The picture he missed from the wall.
"What, moving?" the janitor said.
"Your rent is paid three months ahead!"
"What good is the flat?"
Asked poor Louis, "Read that!"
And the janitor smiled as he read:

chorus

Home Sweet Home

'Midst   pleas__ - ures   and

pal - a - ces   Though__   we   may

roam, Be   it   ev - er_____   so

hum - ble, There's   no____   place   like

home!   A   charm__   from____   the

skies   Seems   to   hal____ - low   us

there Which, seek___ through__ the

world, Is ne'er met with else - where.

Home! Home__! Sweet, sweet home! There's

no___ place__ like home__! There's

no___ place like home!

2

I gaze on the moon
As I tread the drear wild,
And feel that my mother
Now thinks of her child;
As she looks on that moon
From our own cottage door
Through the woodbine whose fragrance
Will cheer me no more.

chorus

127

continued next page

3

An exile from home
Splendor dazzles in vain.
Oh, give me my lowly
Thatched cottage again!
The birds singing gaily
That came at my call—
Give me them with the peace of mind
Dearer than all.

chorus

4

How sweet 'tis to sit
'Neath a fond father's smile,
The caress of a mother
To soothe and beguile.
Let others delight
'Midst new pleasures to roam,
But give me, oh, give me
The pleasures of home.

chorus

5

To thence I'll return,
Overburdened with care.
My heart's dearest solace
Will smile on me there.
No more from that cottage
Again will I roam.
Be it ever so humble,
There's no place like home!

chorus